Published by 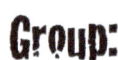 Group:

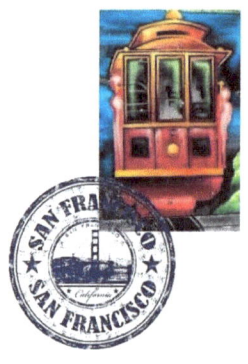 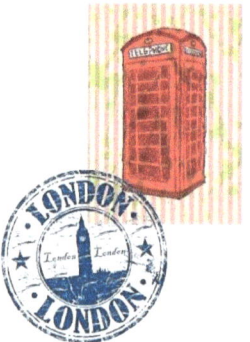 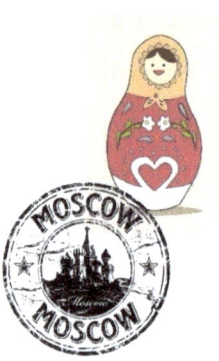

Copyright © 2017 Julie G Fox/Clever Fox Press

All rights reserved. No part of this publication may be reproduced, distributed, or transmitted in any form or by any means, including photocopying, recording, or other electronic or mechanical methods, without the prior written permission of the publisher, except in the case of brief quotations embodied in critical reviews and certain other non-commercial uses permitted by copyright law.

For permission requests, write to the publisher, addressed "Attention: Permissions Coordinator," at julie@cleverfoxpress.com

Ordering Information:
Quantity sales. Special discounts are available on quantity purchases by corporations, associations, and others. For details, contact the publisher at the address above.

Publisher's Cataloguing-in-Publication Data:
The Cats of the Hermitage
Fox, Julie G.
Klot, Masha
Bulbeck, Leonora
Cover Image & Title Page Image: Vergasova, Yana (DepositPhotos)

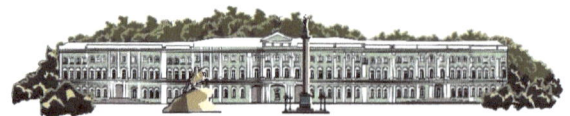

The Cats of the Hermitage

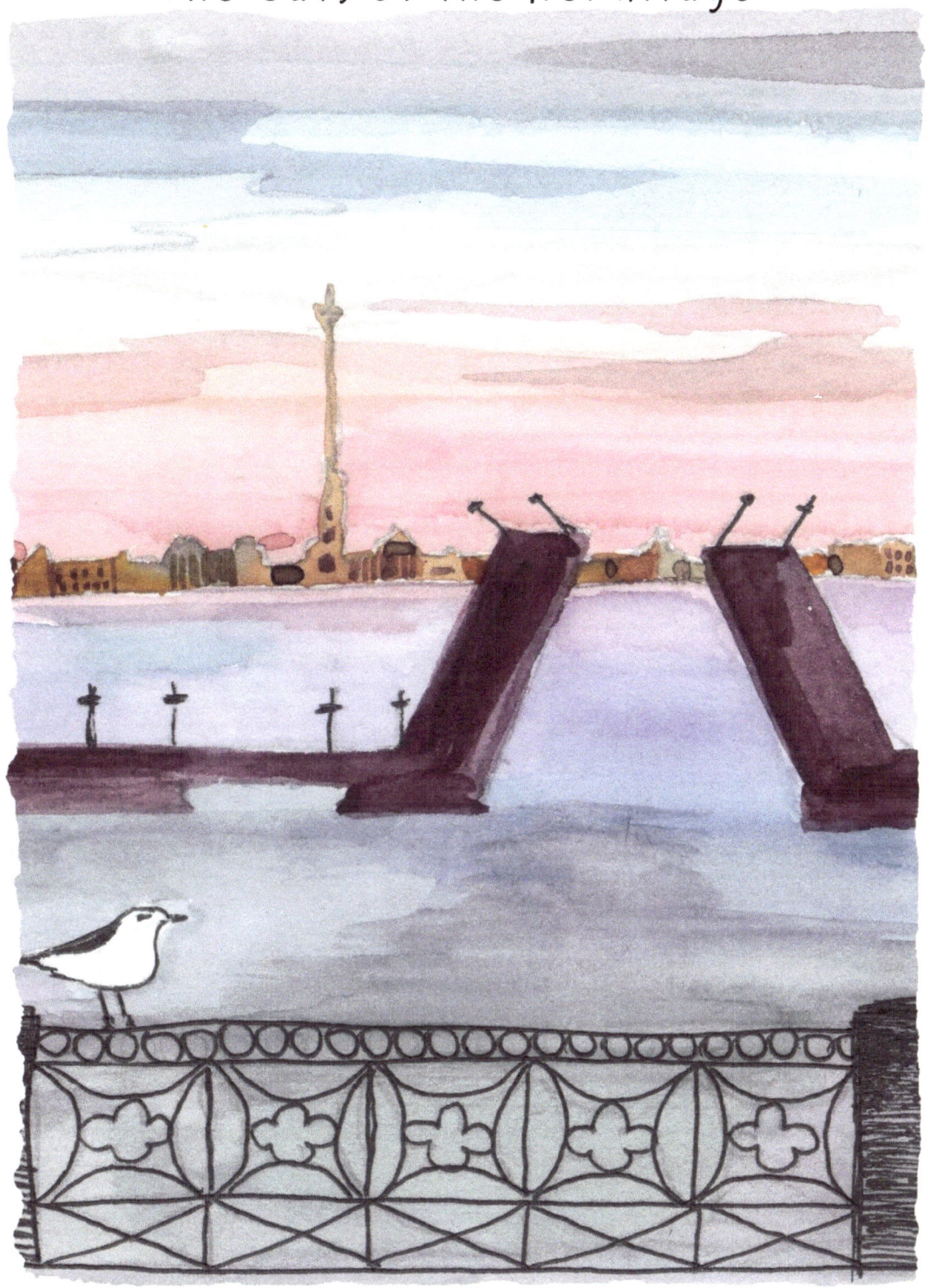

Julie G Fox & Masha Klot

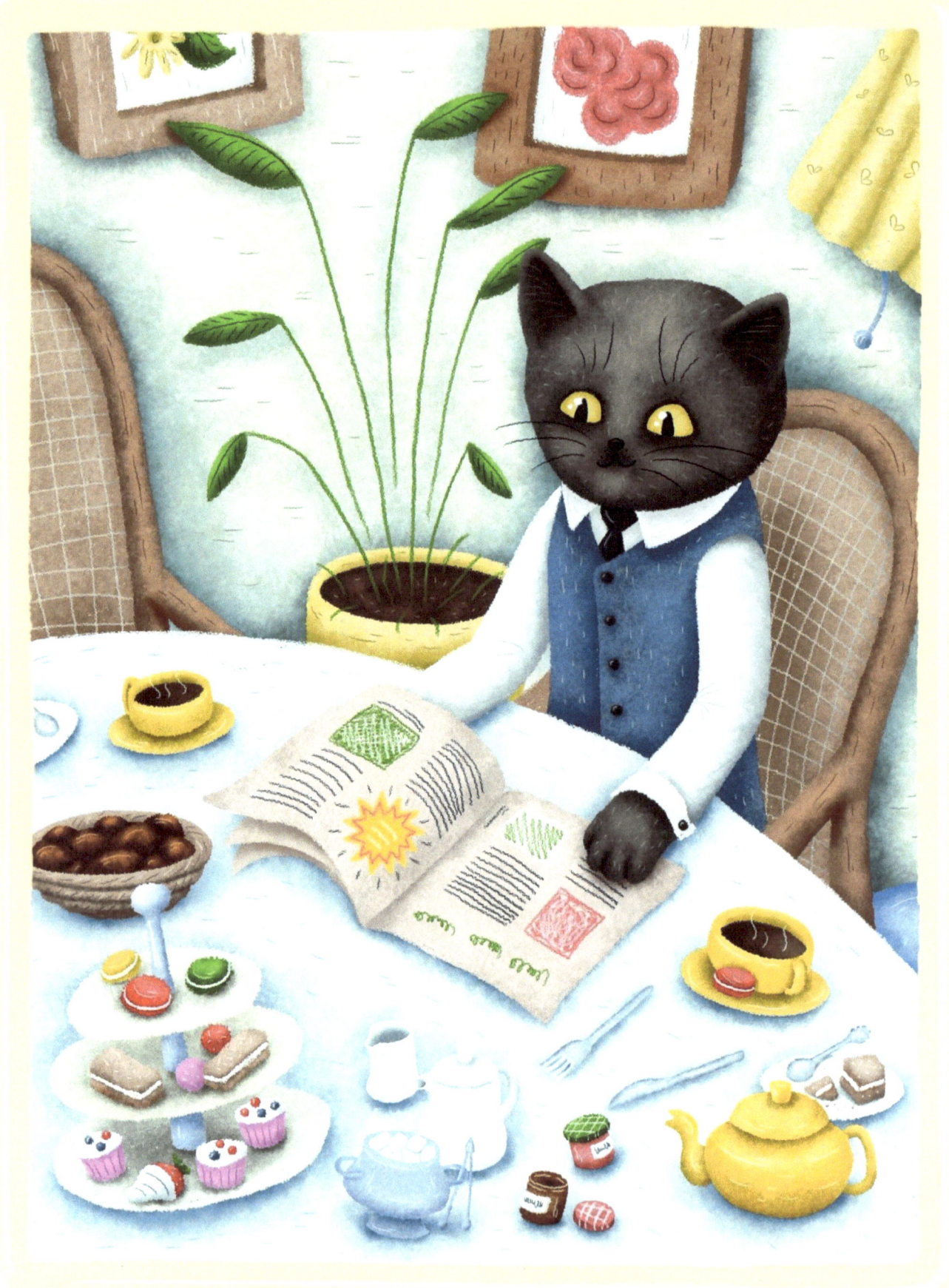

It all started when I, Tommy the Learned Cat, saw an advert in our school's magazine:

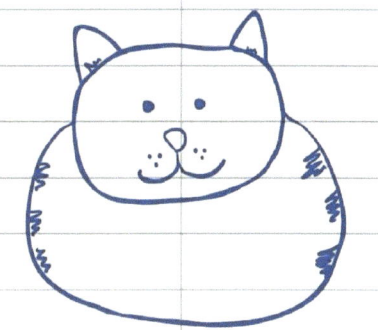

CITY HERALD

CAREER OPPORTUNITY

Are you planning to study art, history or languages at university?
Are you looking for an exciting gap year?
Would you like to get your first work experience
in one of the most famous art museums in the world?
Are you good at catching mice?

If you answered *meow* to all those questions, contact us!

This is not your average gap-year experience. Join other professional felines (providing mouse-catching services to one of the most famous art museums in the world since 1745) at the Hermitage Museum in St Petersburg, Russia!

Your exciting internship year will culminate in the Day of the Hermitage Cat, when you will be presented with an honorary certificate.

Have fun making new friends! Learn or improve your Russian!
Speak to the local cats in *their* language!
A comfy blanket and three meals a day are all included in the package,
as well as free medical care for all your feline health concerns.

APPLY TODAY

City mayor announces

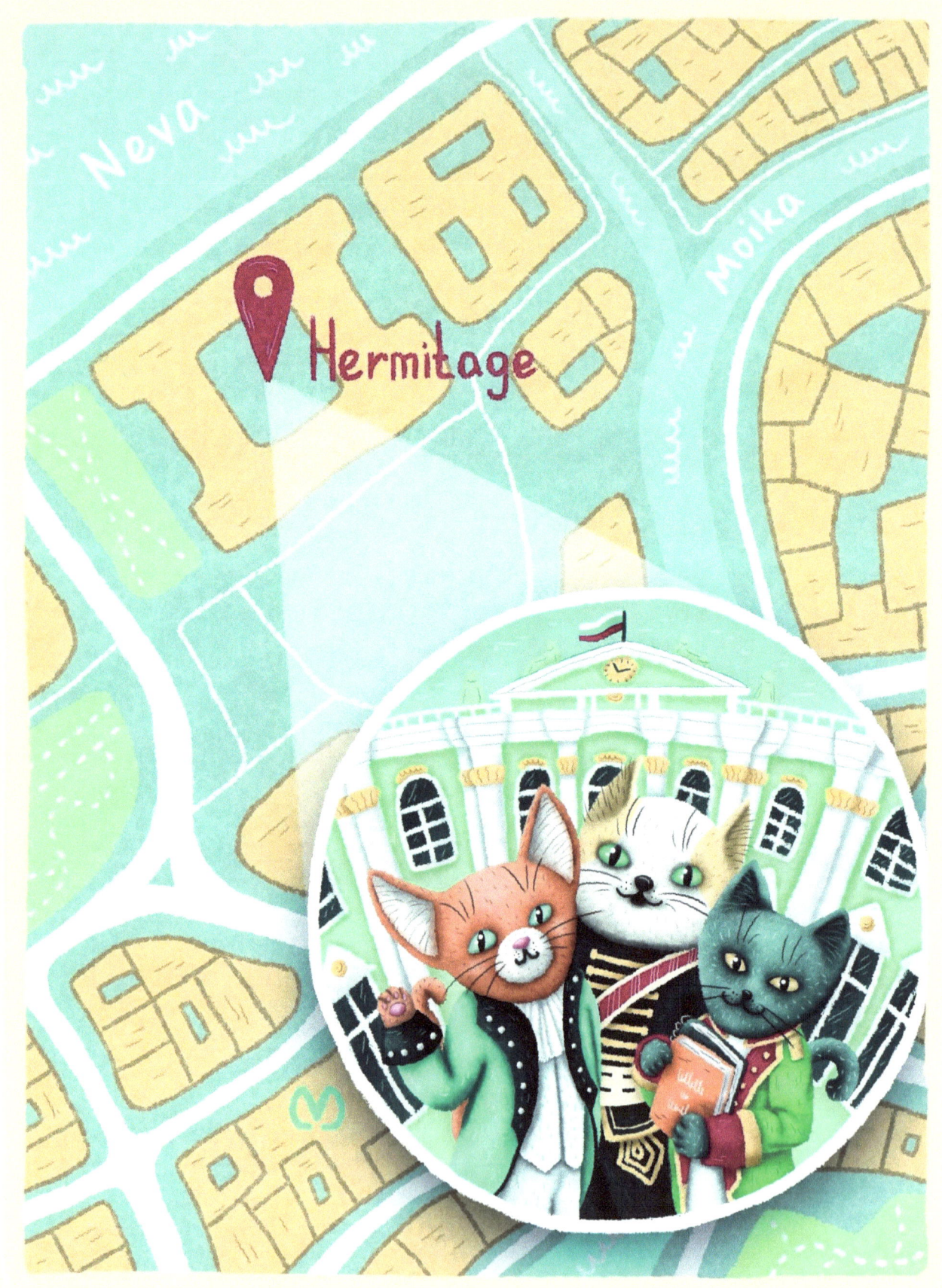

Well, let's just say that I ran home that day to show the advert to Mum and Dad. They, of course, thought this was a terrific idea. What better place to spend my gap year after taking A-levels in art, history and Russian! And so it was decided that I would be going to St Petersburg to work at the Hermitage.

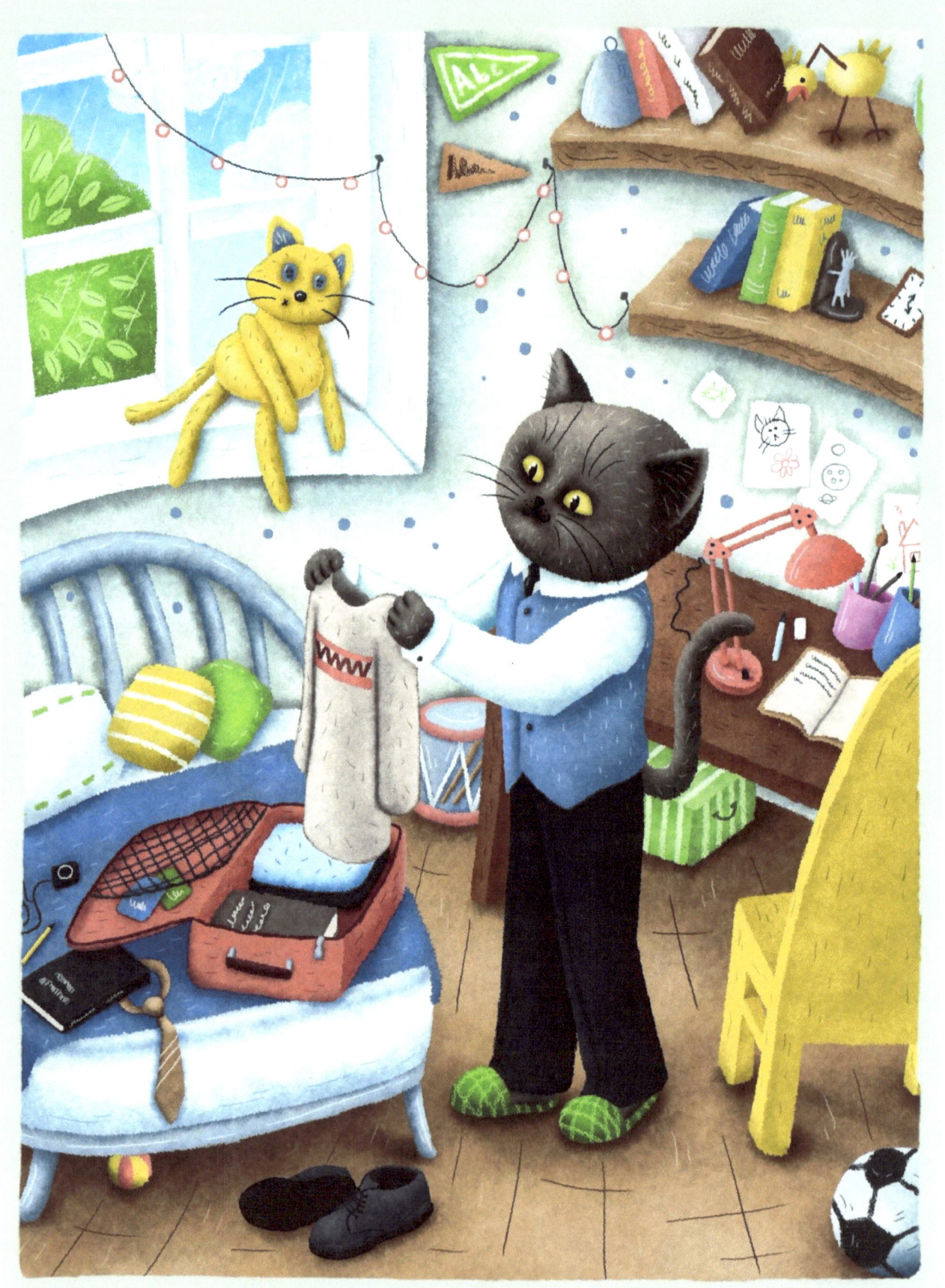

It's a well-documented fact that St Petersburg's Hermitage in Russia, one of the largest and most famous art museums in the world, is home to a huge collection of the most amazing pieces of art. And apparently an army of cats! These professional felines have been guarding the museum's treasures from rodent predators since 1745. Empress Elizaveta, daughter of Peter the Great, signed a decree ordering cats to be found and brought to her court from all over the country.

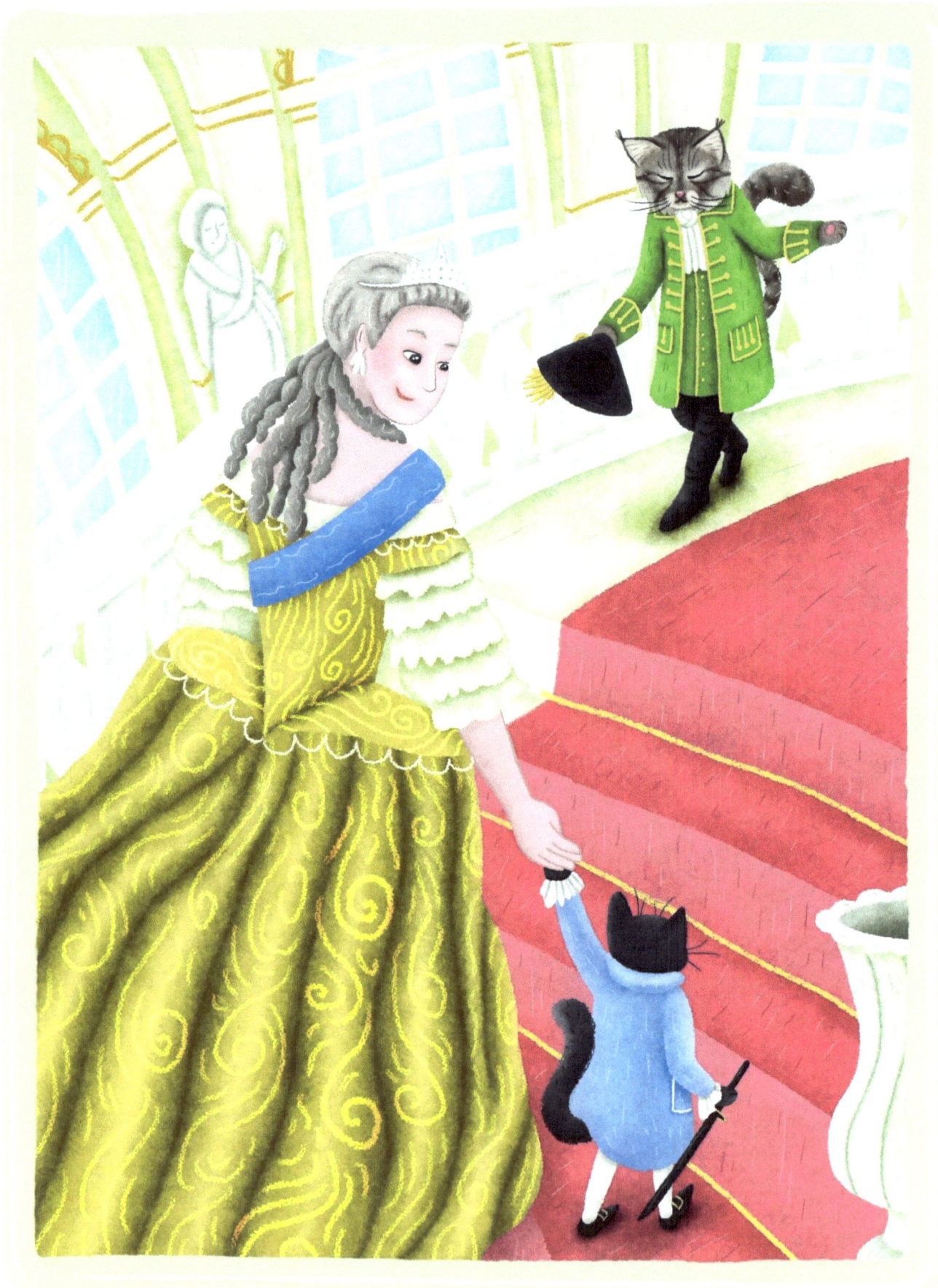

Decree

To find in the city of Kazan the local breeds of the best and the largest of thirty cats, able to catch mice, and accompanied by a person who will look after their health. The cats are to be shipped to St Petersburg to the court of Her Imperial Majesty.

And if anyone has such treasured cats, they should be prepared for a speedy departure in three days from the publication of this decree. The non-declaration of such cats will incur a heavy fine.

Her Imperial Majesty
Elizaveta

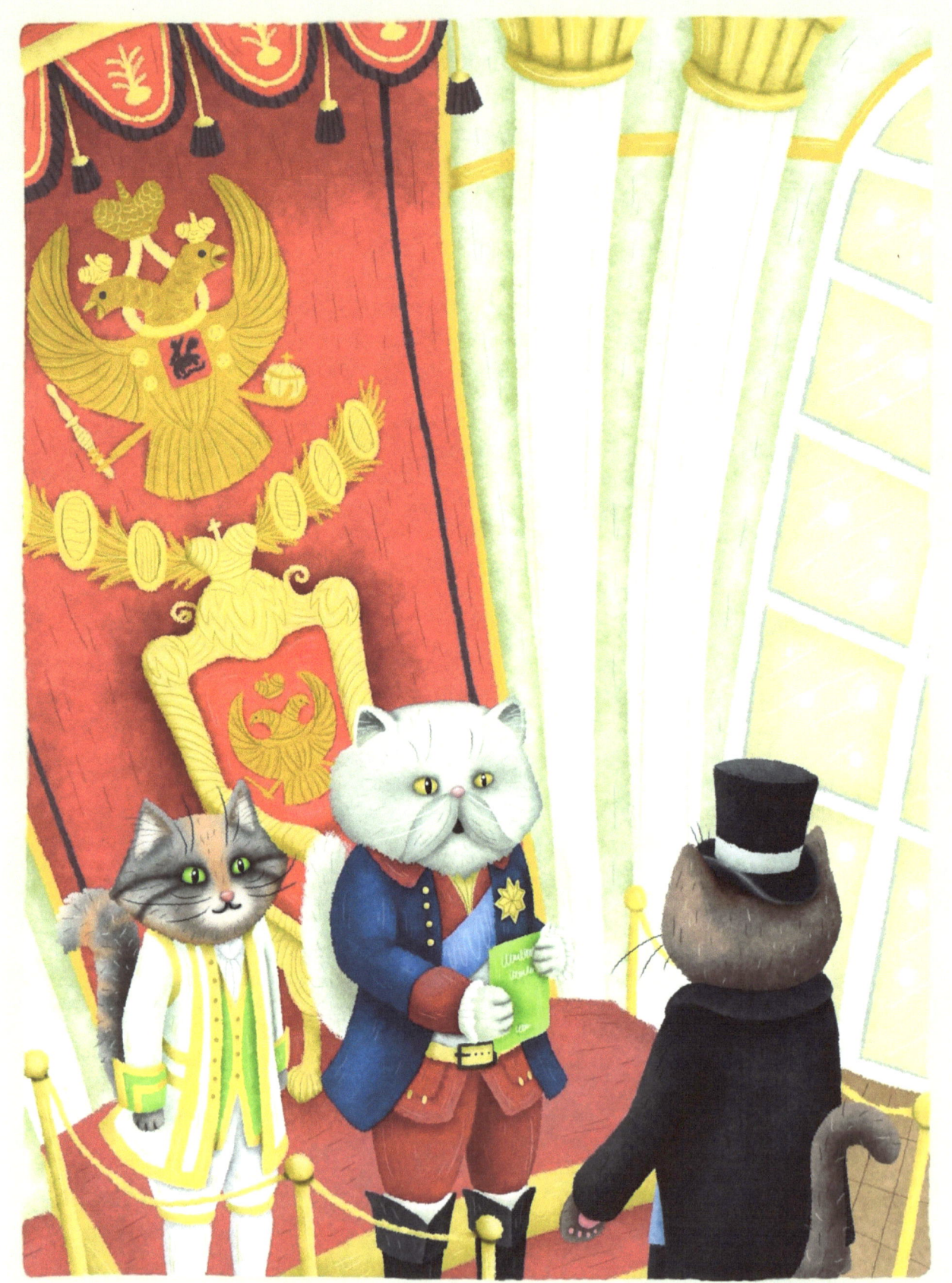

When I arrived in St Petersburg and reported to the Cat Headquarters in the Hermitage's basement, I was told that I would be joining the other seventy cats residing in the museum. Each cat has a passport with its photograph, name and a description of its coat. So my picture was taken along with my paw print to accompany the picture, and I received the most amazing document I have ever sniffed in my entire life with the stamp of the Hermitage Museum on it. The passport said that I was officially an employee of the Hermitage Museum. How exciting!

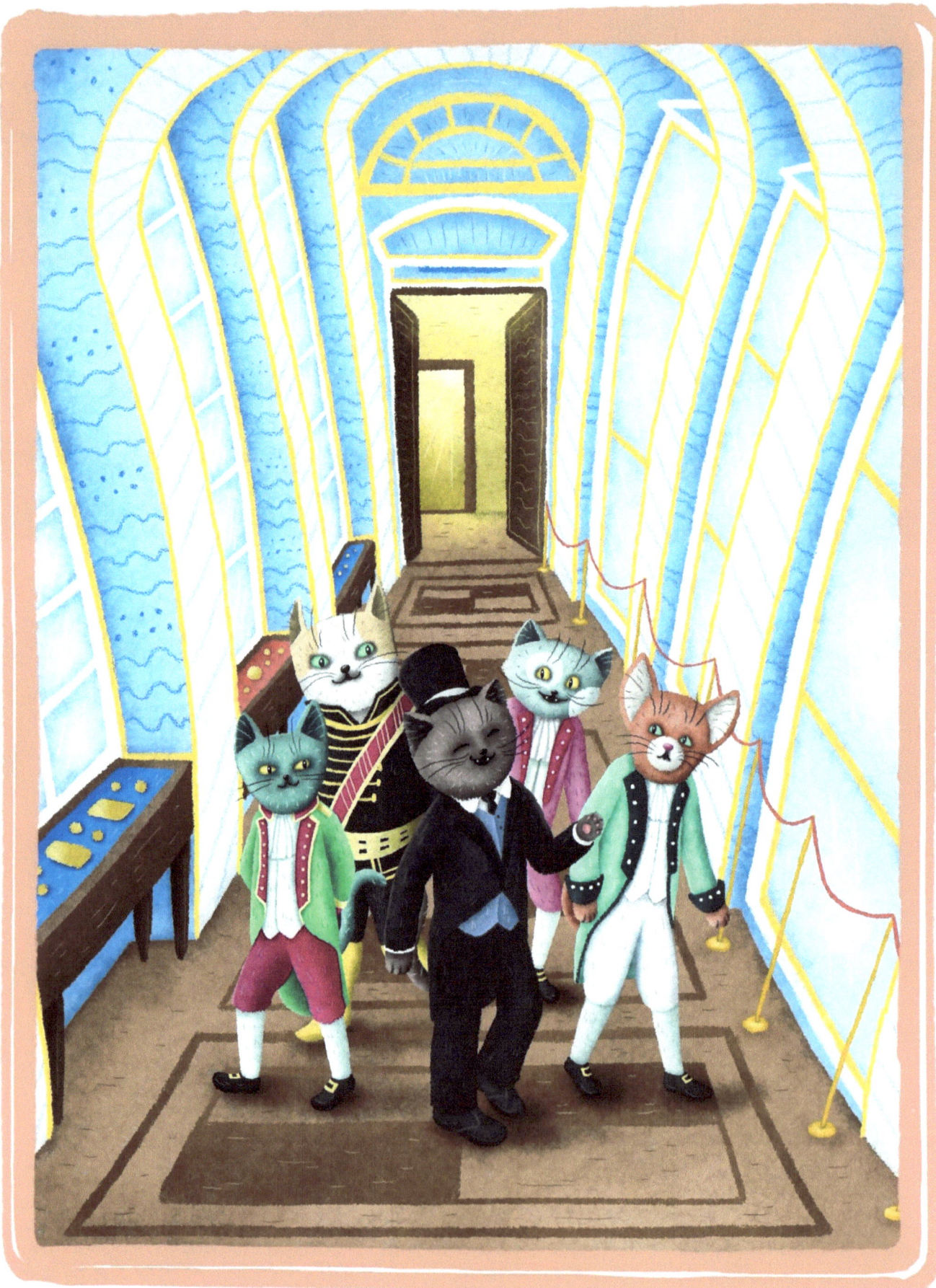

I met other cats on that same day, all different breeds and colours.

And thanks to my A-level in Russian, I was able to speak to them and talk about myself and the country I came from. I told them about the amazing art museums we have in Great Britain (the British Museum, National Gallery, Victoria and Albert Museum, Tate Britain and others) and how I often go there to admire the pieces of art on display and to catch an occasional mouse threatening those museums' collections.

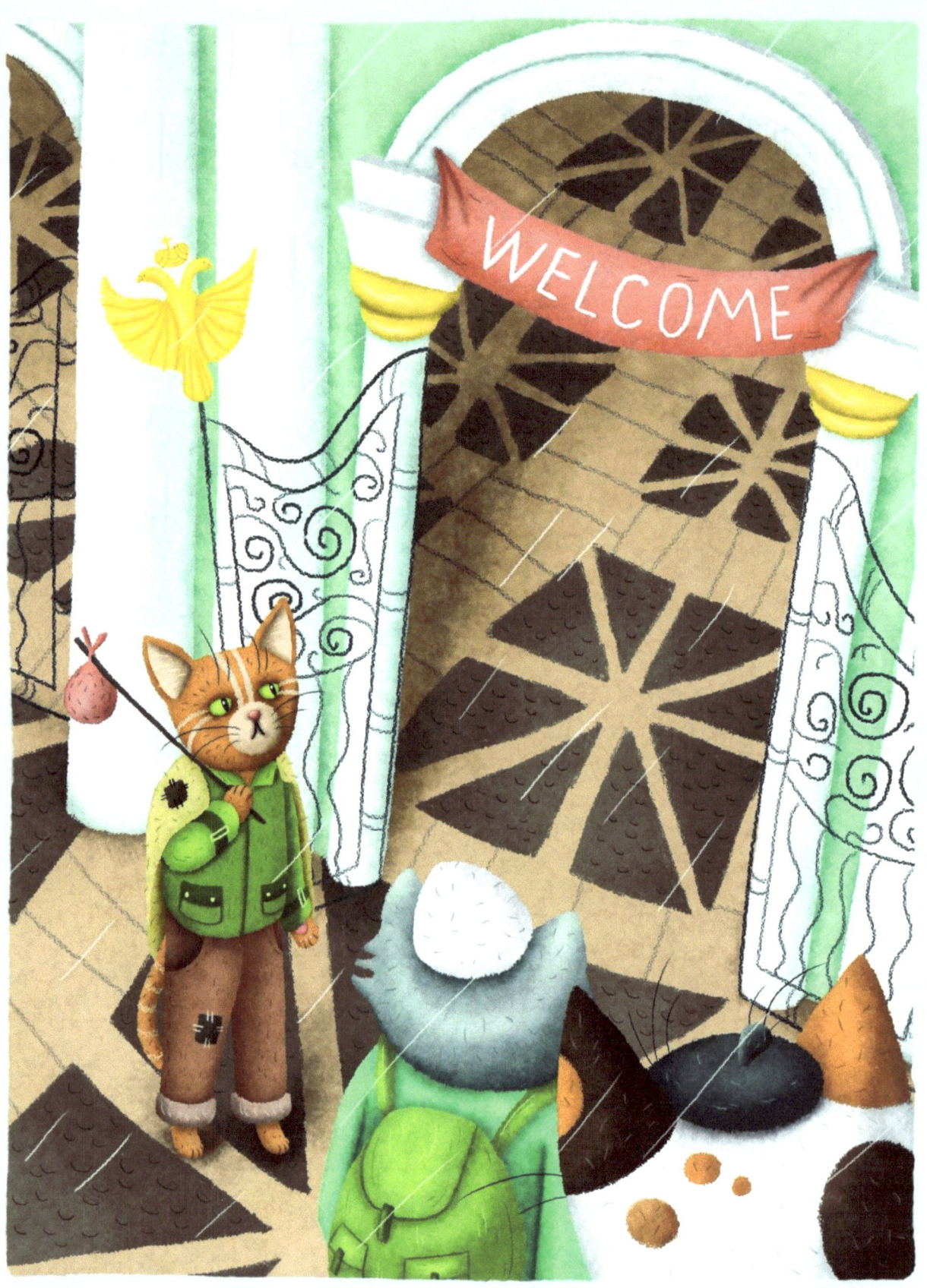

The cats told me all about their life and work and how the Hermitage is famous for not turning away a single stray cat that walks through its doors. All cats are welcome. Those retiring from faithful service to the museum are all rehomed to good families. And they also receive a special certificate (something to brag about to family and friends).

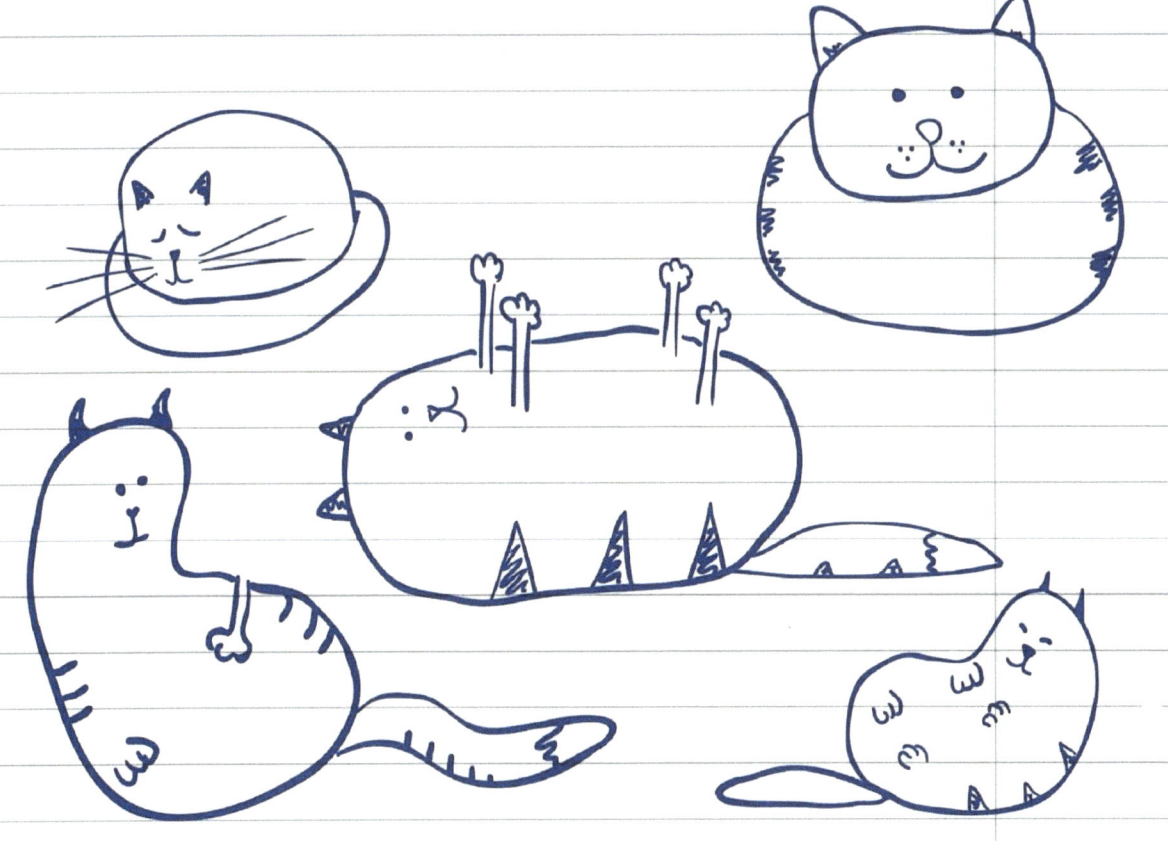

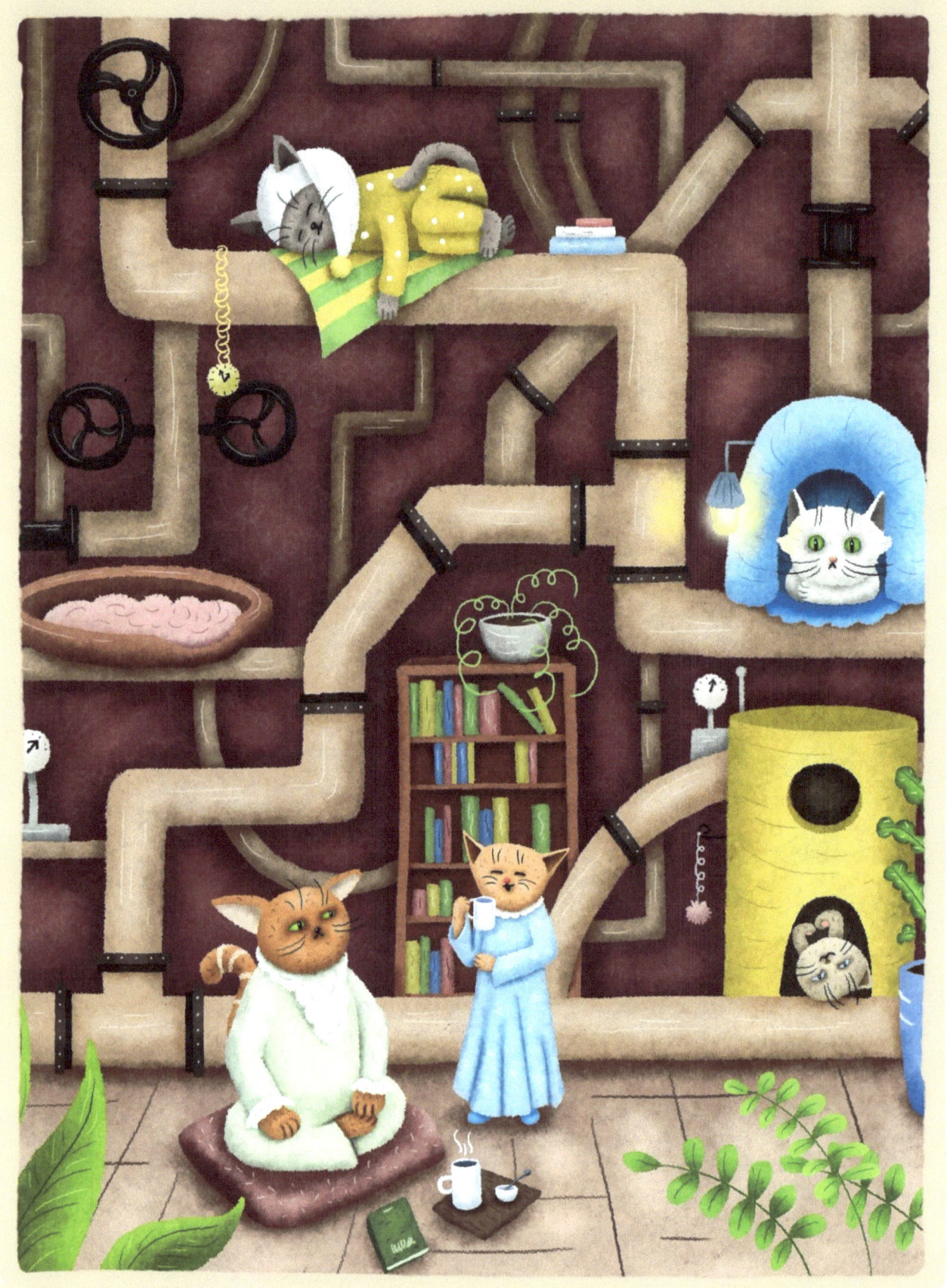

My new colleagues told me that they don't get paid for their work. But they receive much more than that! A roof over their heads, food and the honour of being called a Hermitage Cat. Many doors in the museum have small flaps in them so the cats can come and go as they please between the gardens and the basement. This is where the main offices are. The cats take their naps there and eat their meals. There is even a separate sick bay.

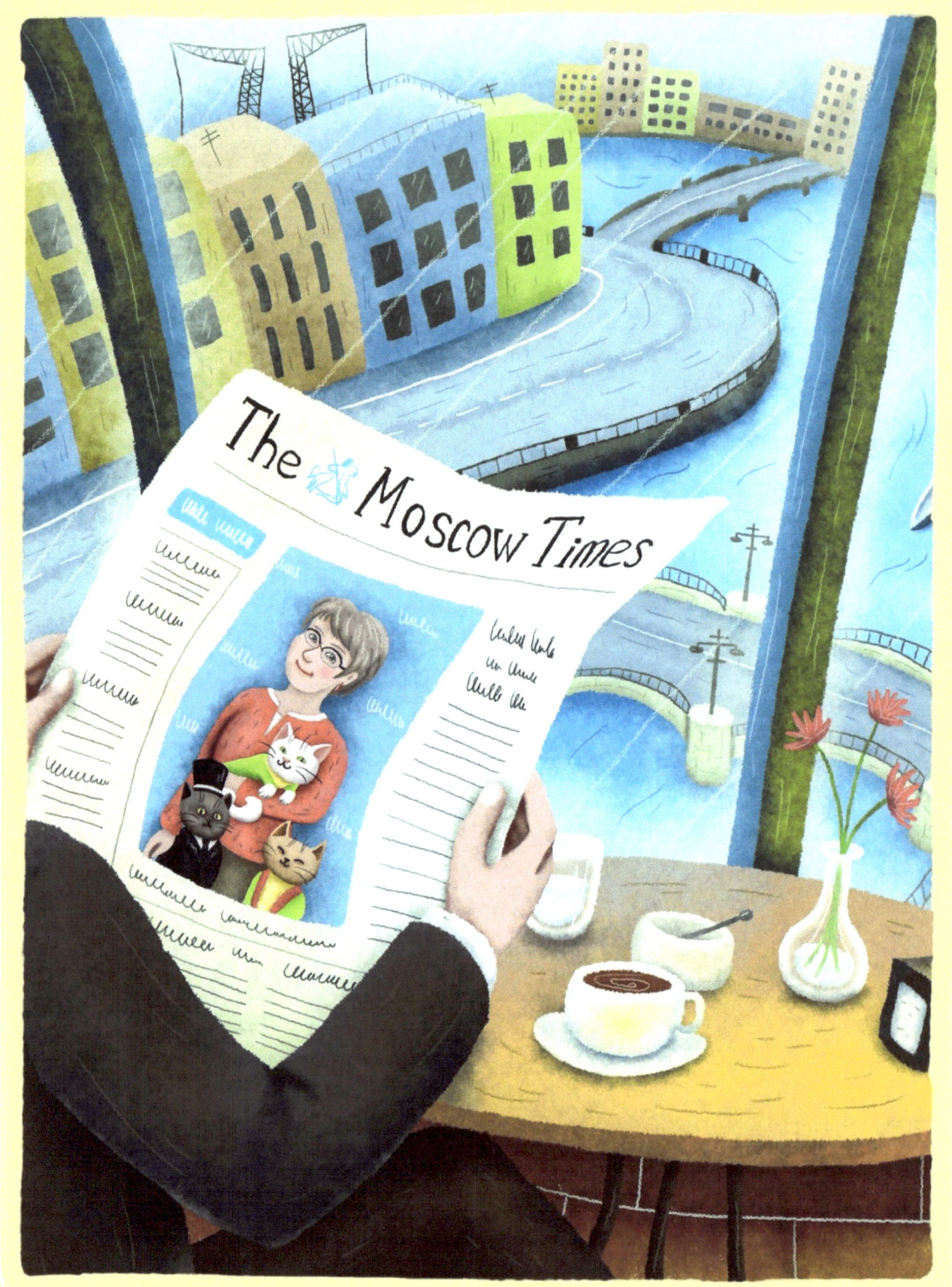

There are special humans looking after the cats. And the cats even have their own press secretary, Miss Maria, who was the first person to introduce me to the museum and to teach me the ropes of my new job. By the way, the day I arrived she was giving an interview to The Moscow Times newspaper. The reporter snapped a picture of me with Miss Maria and my new co-workers. I now keep that issue in my drawer.

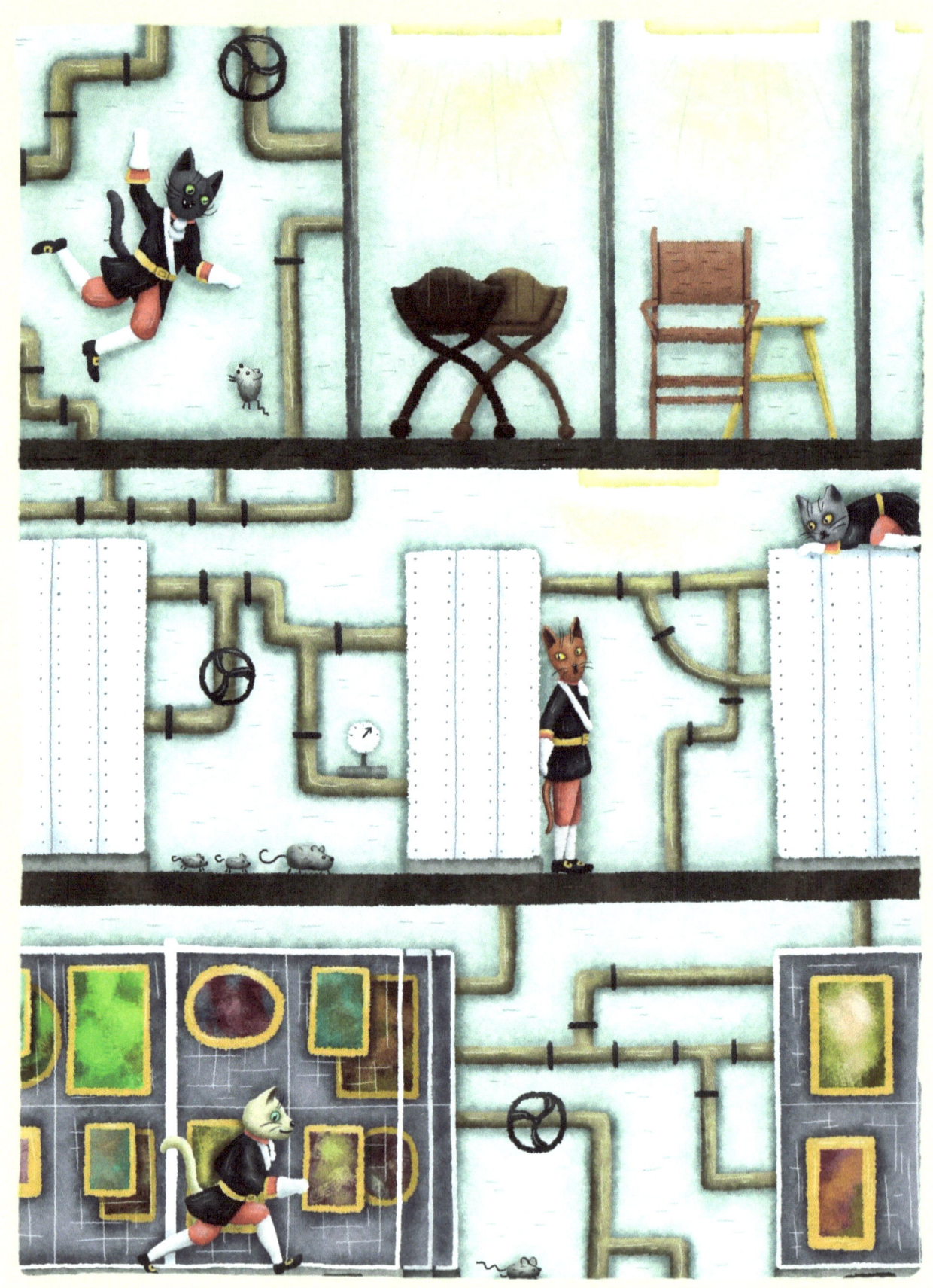

Miss Maria explained to the reporter that the visitors to the museum think that the cats walking about are just your average felines who wake up from their naps and take casual strolls. But they are not! They are the protectors of art! And I, Tommy the Learned Cat, am so lucky to have joined others on the undercover mission to protect the museum's three million treasures. You see, only some of these amazing art pieces are on display. The rest are kept in storage in the basement. And here is where the army of cats (myself included) come in. They patrol the basement and galleries and drive away the sneaky rodents that cause damage to the valuable pieces.

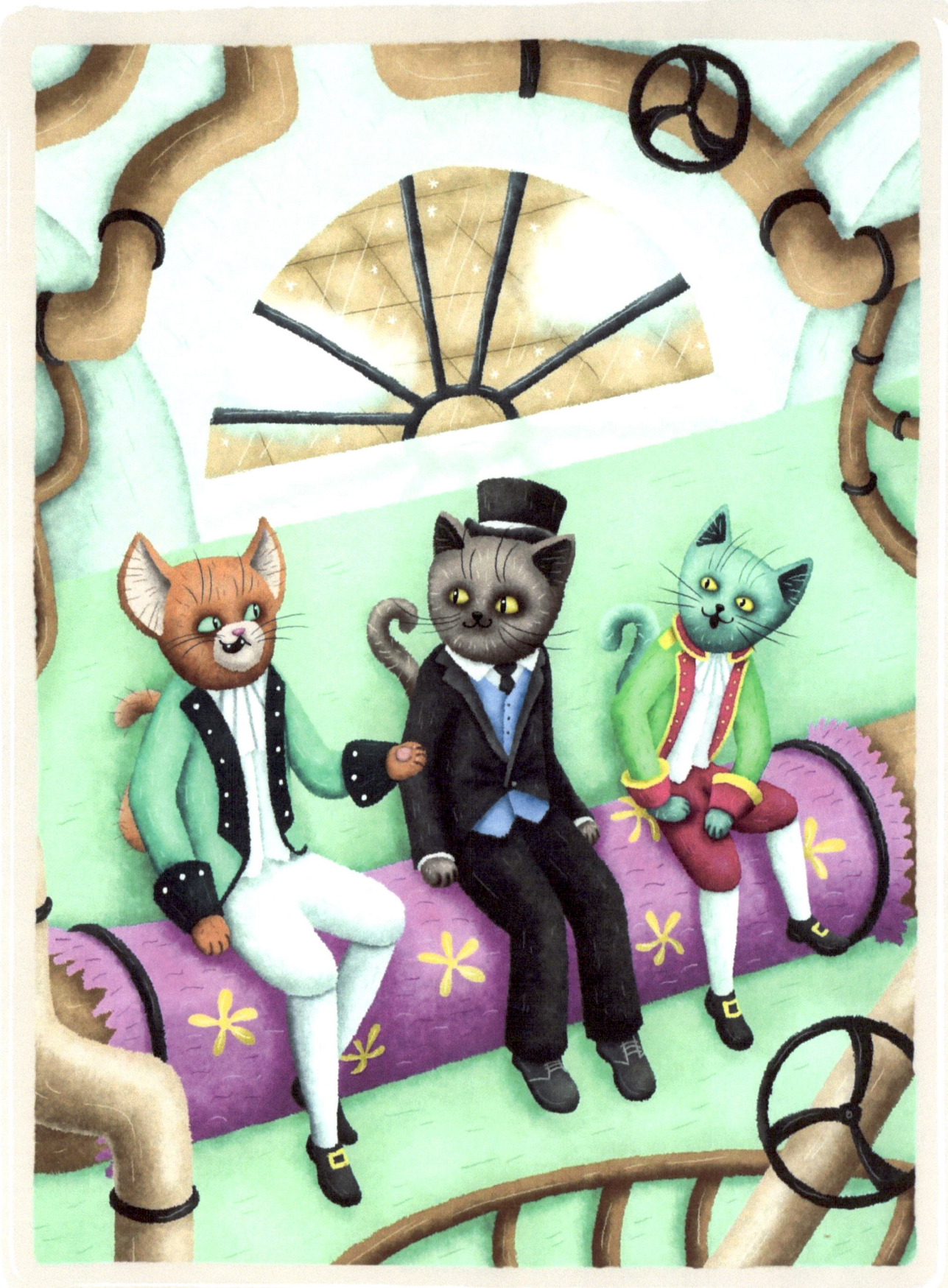

My only concern when I arrived was whether the Hermitage had good heating down in the basements during those famously cold Russian winters. But Miss Maria assured me that the heating was really good, and not one cat ever complained that they didn't enjoy a nice cosy nap by the radiators in the cellars of the famous Winter Palace, the home of the museum.

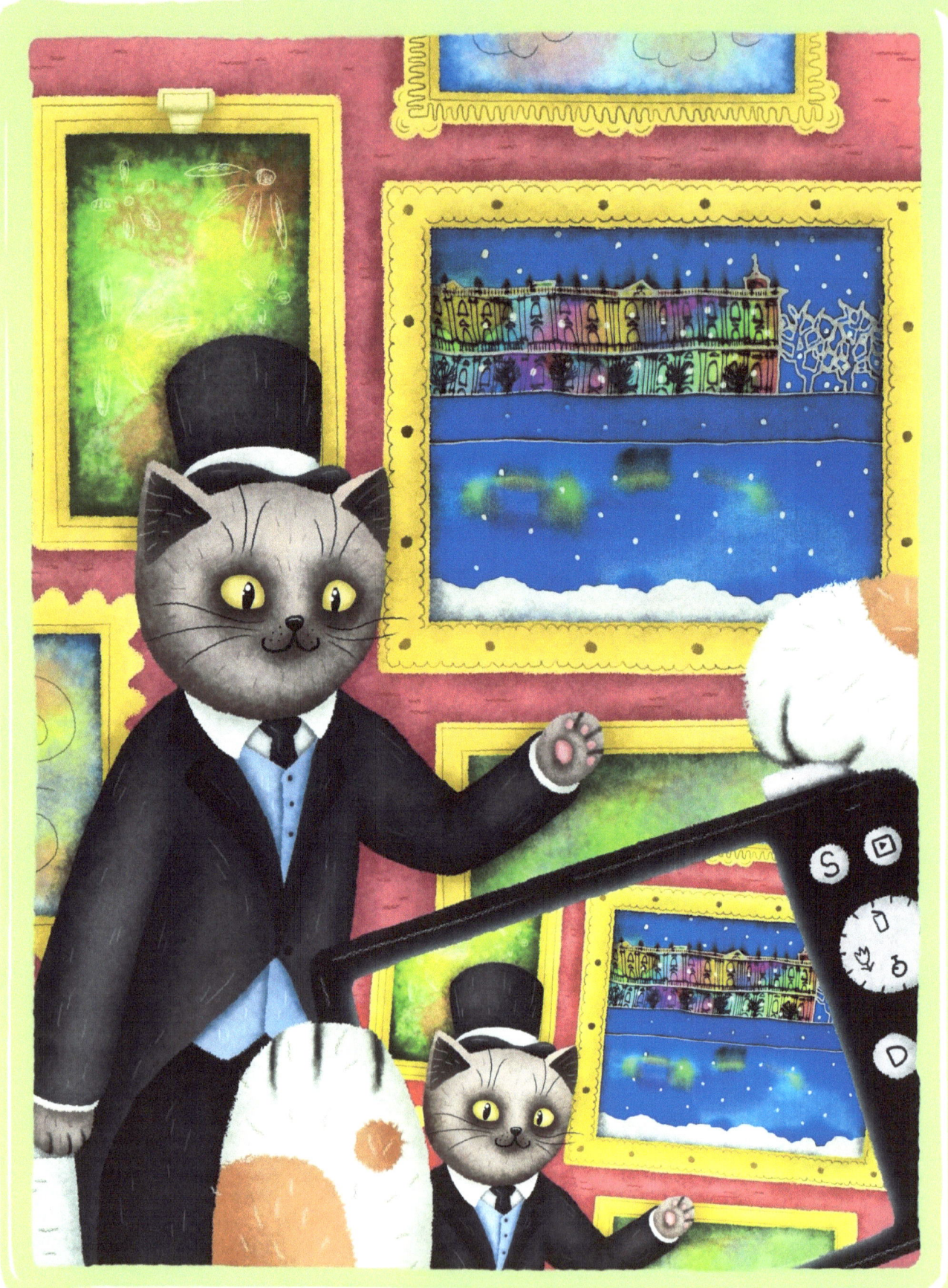

Oh, I forgot to tell you one of the fun bits! There was an art contest held for the local children and pets (cats are great at art too, you know!). Winter nights in St Petersburg can be awfully long so I got myself some art supplies ... and here it is! My Russian-inspired masterpiece: 'Hermitage' by Tommy the Learned Cat. It didn't win the first prize, but my painting was displayed in one of the galleries of the museum with a proper label, just like all the other Hermitage exhibits. What an honour! I was very proud to snap a picture of it and send it to Mum and Dad, who couldn't believe their eyes.

Here is my special certificate, which I received from Miss Maria at the end of that amazing year in St Petersburg.

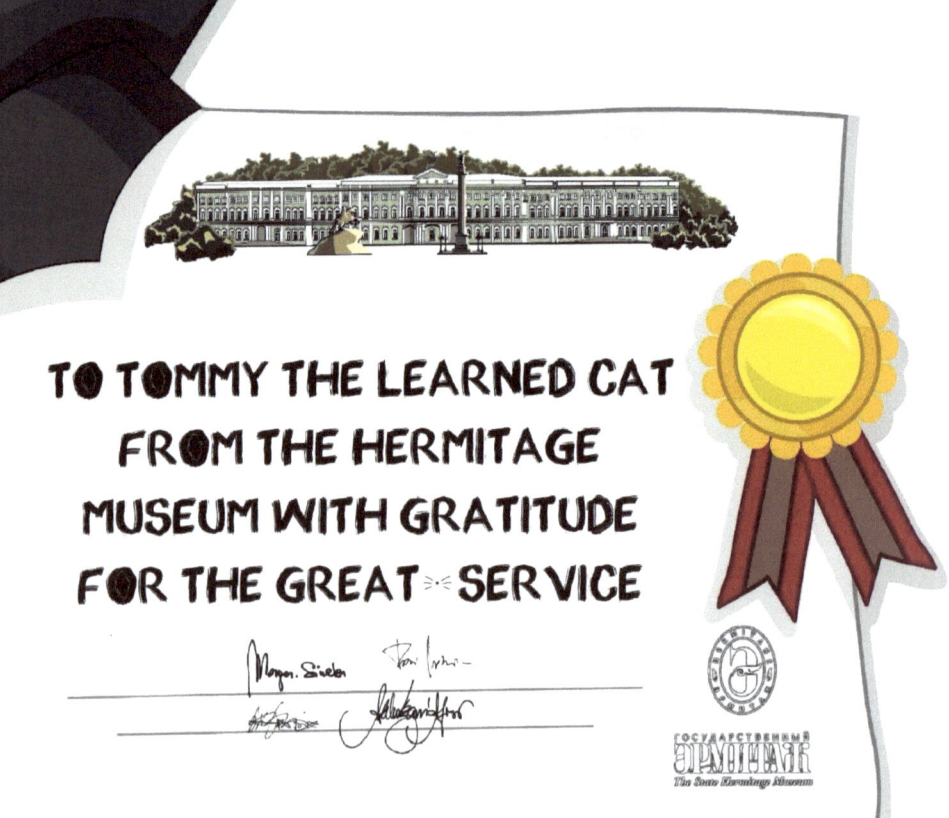

TO TOMMY THE LEARNED CAT FROM THE HERMITAGE MUSEUM WITH GRATITUDE FOR THE GREAT SERVICE

It now hangs on the wall next to my other important achievements, like 'Rugby School's Mouse Catcher of the Year', 'Diploma in Purring Therapy', 'Grade 8 Certificate in Cuddle Time' and the most important one, of course, 'The Best Pet Diploma'.

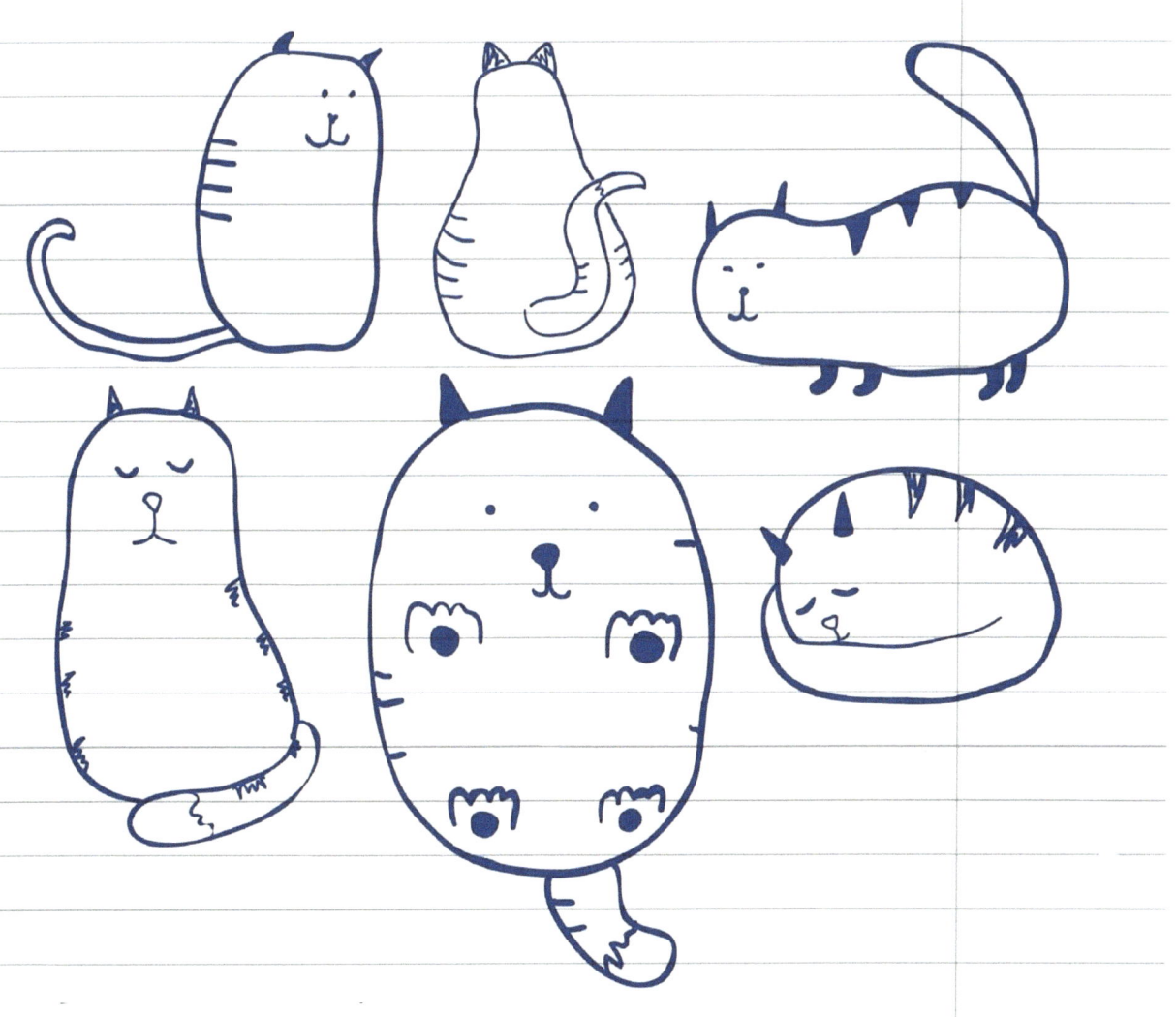

The End

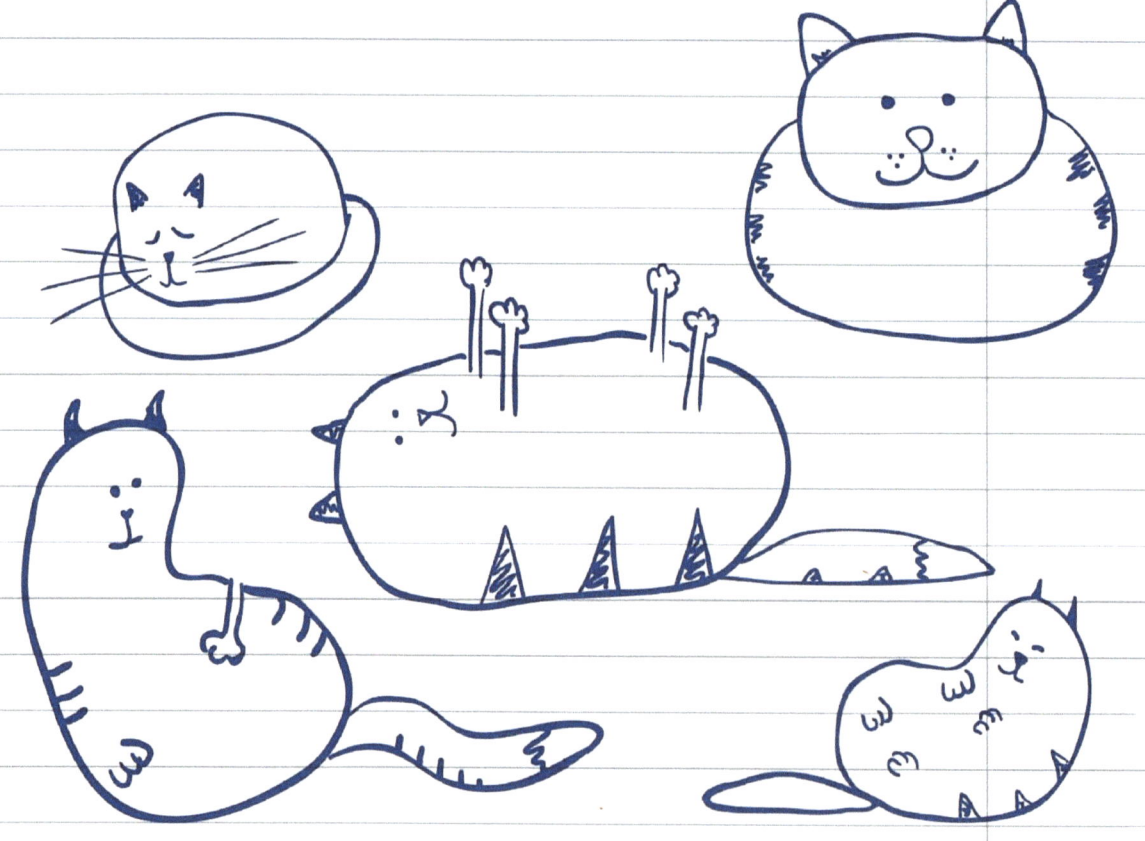

www.ingramcontent.com/pod-product-compliance
Lightning Source LLC
Chambersburg PA
CBHW051826210526
45473CB00005B/1754